RUNNING FROM
GOD

BY
MONICA R. HAYES

TABLE OF CONTENT

DEDICATION

i

This book is dedicated to my mother, Helga Vogt Hayes.

"My role model for how I live my life. She was my strength, taught me tenacity, and endurance. My mom left my family with a legacy of love and respect. You are forever in my heart, Moni."

INTRODUCTION

As I started my journey of understanding who God is, my conversations with people about who God is and isn't in their lives gave me the inspiration to write. The struggle was the same "running from God", not realizing how "running to God" changes lives. The common theme was and still is the belief that we all have a purpose. The challenge is to identify with confidence and assurance what that purpose is.

I based my book on Jonah, who ran entirely in the opposite direction from what God had directed. Just like us, we can't see beyond our own desires. We run from God in many ways. We know situations and circumstances aren't how we hoped for, always searching for something and trying to fill a gap. In conversation with relatives, friends, co-workers, and associates from different cultures and backgrounds, the challenge and struggle are the same. I truly believe we all have similar wants and desires to be fulfilled, happy, have peace of mind, the ability and means to provide and care for self and loved ones, have good health, and a healthy, meaningful relationship with that special person.

The question is: "How do we get there?" The answer is easy; it requires a commitment, renewing our minds and changing how we think. Whether we accept it or not, the fulfillment of our current and future lives comes from God. His plan and purpose for every soul on earth is for good, and we must choose.

The choice is a very personal decision.

THE BEGINNING OF THE JOURNEY

From the beginning, our direction is pre-determined and in motion. (Jeremiah 1:1-5) The Word of the Lord came to me, saying, "Before I formed you in the womb, I knew you; before you were born, I set you apart: I appointed you as a prophet to the nation." The direction was established and set in motion before conception. We can't choose our journey, but we can determine how we travel the journey.

Jonah chose his direction and almost lost his life and the lives of others. He became bitter and resentful.

Let God have His way, running to and not running from Him. We may not tell anyone or talk about the internal confusion and emptiness that never seems satisfied. We hear and read about how other lives have changed, but what about my life? It's our thinking and strong will to have it our way. I did, and, at times, still do, struggle to let go of my independent ways of thinking. Believing that we have complete control over our lives. We only have God's best when we trust Him and let Him have control of our lives. God's plan and purpose provide all we need: courage, strength, true identity, and confidence that no person or amount of money can alter. He gives us the desires of our hearts according to His word. The first paragraph in the book of John tells us the importance of understanding God's word. John 1: 1- 4…."1) In the beginning was the Word, and the Word was with God, and the Word was God. 2)

The same was in the beginning with God. 3) All things were made by him; and without him was not anything made that was made. 4) In him was life, and the life was the light of men."

Many people in the body of Christ (the church) are hurting and have lost faith in believing for the better. People have gone through intense and unbelievable hardships, loss, and pain that they have forgotten who God is and struggle to still believe what He can do. Times may be difficult, and life may change, but God has and will never change who he is. Hebrews 13:8 (KJV) tells us, "Jesus Christ the same yesterday, today, and forever." God has not forgotten about us, but we forget about Him. We run to a better job with more pay, a bigger house, and a better car, and we look for a husband or wife; we run to everything but our "source." Everything we need and want is in Him. God is our supplier, and He knows everything about us: our desires, our future, our hopes, and our dreams.

This book speaks very clearly to my spirit and heart as I complete it. It gives me an understanding of the challenges and struggles I face trying to find my purpose and stay in the perfect will of God. In the book of Joshua 24:15, it tells us, "But if serving the Lord seems undesirable to you, then choose for yourselves this day whom you will serve." We can't do anything without the help of God; it all comes from Him.

John 15:5: "I am the vine; you are the branches. If you remain in me and I in you, you will bear much fruit; apart from me, you can do nothing".

The journey to find purpose is one of the most significant challenges in life. It is also the most rewarding, but it takes work. It's not hard, but it's work - work to build a relationship with Him as we build relationships with people. It takes effort to know someone, understand them, make compromises, and accept them for who they are. It takes the same effort to build up faith and trust in God. Just as natural relationships have challenges, there are challenges when you choose to follow after Jesus. Good and evil are ever-present; it's a constant battle, but a battle worth fighting. There's nothing new about following Christ; it takes dedication and commitment. Scriptures tell us that if we seek the kingdom of God first, then all these things will be added to us. When we put God ahead of everything in our lives, we will see him working through all circumstances and events for our good. Whether you are just beginning to seek God or you have been a Christian for years, we should never stop seeking to know God at a deeper level. Hebrews 11:6 in the New International Version (NIV) of the Bible reads: "And without faith it is impossible to please God, because anyone who comes to him must believe that he exists and that he rewards those who earnestly seek him"1. Hebrews 11:1-6 NIV describes faith as "confidence in what we hope for and assurance about what we do not see"2. The passage also explains that "by faith we understand that the universe was formed at God's command, so that what is seen was not made out of what was visible"2.

Whenever you make up your mind to change and do the will of God, LOOK OUT! I thought this book would be about being hardheaded and strong-willed, but I realize it combines strong will and fighting against God. God will never go against our will, and it doesn't matter how you pray and fast. he will not. God gives you the freedom to choose.

We fight against our divine purpose when we struggle with the will and way of God, letting God have His way, running to Him, and not running from Him. We may run differently, but the result can be devastating and painfully long. The verses in Isaiah describe how God works; it tells us, Isaiah 55:8-8 "For my thoughts are not your thoughts, neither are your ways my ways, "declares the Lord. 9 "As the heavens are higher than the earth, so are my ways higher than your way and my thoughts than your thoughts. 10 As the rain and the snow come down from heaven, and do not return to it without watering the earth and making it bud and flourish, so that it yields seed for the sower and bread for the eater, 11 so is my word that goes out from my mouth: It will not return unto me empty, but will accomplish what I desire and achieve the purpose for which I sent."

I learned through my experiences and understanding of how our will creates chaos and will brings about unwanted circumstances and situations when we're not aligned with God's plan. God is all-knowing of who we are and our day-to-day lives; in Revelation 22:13, the Lord says, "I am the Alpha and the Omega, the First and the Last, the Beginning and the End." God knows us better than anyone, including our parents; Jeremiah 1:5 "Before I formed you in the womb I knew you, before you were born I set you apart." Just in case there is any doubt about how God knows us, there are many scriptures to tell us the in-depth of God's knowledge of who we are; one I love is Psalms 139. Psalms 139: 1-5Z says, "You have searched me, Lord, and you know me.2 You know when I sit and rise, you perceive my thoughts from afar.3 You discern my going out and lying down; you are familiar with all my ways. 4 Before a word is on my tongue, you, Lord, know it completely.5 You hem me in behind and before. You lay your hand upon me". Psalms 139:13, 15 &-16 adds even more clarity; "For you created my inmost being; you knit me together in my mother's womb. 15 My frame was not hidden from you when I was made in the secret place, when I was woven together in the depths of the earth. 16 Your eyes saw my unformed body; all the days ordained for me were written in your book before one of them came to be".

Be assured of one thing: God loves you unconditionally. Period!! Nothing in our lives is a surprise to Him; it's only a surprise to us. He knew and knows the outcome. God loves us so much and wants only the best for us. Thank God; He is faithful and always there waiting for us to ask for His help. I hope you begin to comprehend and understand the depth of God's love as you continue to read. If you've let life move you away from God's love, I hope you will return to Him. If you don't know Him and have been apprehensive about who He is, I hope you will ask Him into your life. Let God control your present and future to have what God has just for you entirely. Matthew 7:7-8 says: "Ask, and it will be given to you; seek, and you will find; knock, and the door will be opened to you." For everyone who asks receives; the one who seeks finds; and to the one who knocks, the door will be opened". You have nothing to lose and everything to gain when you have Jesus. It doesn't matter who you are, how important you are, where you come from, or where you've been. God is the answer, as you will read in the following chapters.

To complete the journey with success, we have to accept the discomfort of change and be determined to commit to the process. The process can be painful; God is the potter and reshapes us repeatedly until He is satisfied with how He wants us. Jeremiah 18:3-4, Then I went down to the potter's house, and there He was, making something on the wheel. 4 But the vessel that He was making of clay was spoiled in the hand of the potter; so He remade it into another vessel, as it pleased the potter to make".

COMMITMENTS GOD REQUIRES

Some changes have to be mastered along the journey of change. These changes are what God requires of us to have the ability to renew our minds to God's way of thinking. You can't operate in these commitments without a renewed mind (willingness to change) and willingness to follow God's requirements in the form of commands. There are several; here are three commandments that help us change our thinking and lives.

The first commitment of God is LOVE! - God LOVES us and offers us an excellent PLAN for our lives. God's love is so great that John 3:16 describes it like this: "God so loved the world that He gave His one and only Son, that whoever believes in Him shall not perish, but have eternal life." Part of that love is God's plan for us [Christ speaking]: "I came that they might have life, and might have it abundantly" [that it might be full and meaningful- John 10:10, unconditional love.

Our relationship with God is like the loving relationship between a child and a parent. Like a loving parent, God knows and cares deeply for us. Love is the main character and attribute of God. Love is the essential part of his nature. God is love, and all who live in love live in God, and God lives in them. (NLT, 1 John 4:16)

As Christians, we are required to love each other unconditionally, despite all differences and not because of sameness. We are to love so profoundly that love in the bible is called agapao (verb) and agape (noun). It means affection, benevolence, goodwill, high esteem, and concern for the welfare of the loved one. It is deliberate, purposeful love rather than emotional or impulsive love. Almost all New Testament references to love are agapeo or agape in the original Greek. The King James Version of the Bible sometimes translates agape as "charity." Still, charity has now taken on the meaning of assistance to the poor rather than benevolent love. Let me help you fully understand the love God requires.

Noun

1. agape - (Christian theology) the love of God or Christ for humanity

2. agape - selfless love of one person for another without sexual implications (spiritual love)

3. agape - a religious meal shared as a sign of love and fellowship

The Bible has scripture after scripture that describes how we are to love one another with God's kind of love. Love and versions of love are used 610 times in the bible, illustrating its significance. We may not know what love is, but the bible explains what love does: 1 Corinthians 13:4-7. The New International Version; 4) Love is patient, love is kind. It does not envy, it does not boast, it is not proud. 5) It does not dishonor others, it is not self-seeking, it is not easily angered, it keeps no record of wrongs. 6)Love does not delight in evil but rejoices with the truth. 7) It always protects, always trusts, always hopes, always perseveres.

The Israelites were also commanded to have sincere goodwill for each other (NIV, Leviticus 19:18): "Do not seek revenge or bear a grudge against one of your people, but love your neighbor as yourself. I am the LORD".

We demonstrate God's love when we follow the commandment from Deuteronomy 6:5, "And thou shalt love the Lord thy God with all thy heart, with all thy soul, and with all thy might." Loving the Lord means having a relationship with him. You can only have a relationship once you know who you're in a relationship with.

When you learn how to love God, it becomes easy to love others. When you truly love, your heart is pure and open so that you can hear what he is saying to you. When there is no love, the junk in your heart takes over, and you can not hear anything good or accomplish anything good. When your mind is in control, it will make you believe you can control the outcome. If that were true, we would not need GOD because we would be as Almighty as he is.

Love is the most vital force in the universe; it is to feel a passion, devotion, or tenderness for and to take pleasure in. Control, on the other hand, has nothing to do with tenderness or devotion. Control is to regulate, reserve, hold back, and restrain. Love is easy since it gives and receives; control, on the other hand, demands and gives little in return. Love brings success; it opens the door for others to come in.

God will never intrude on your life since He has to be invited in. When He comes, He brings his gentle, loving kindness. Love forgives and accepts others rather than tries to change them. Love doesn't look at faults and flaws; love is tender and kind, compassionate and merciful. Suppose you never have a loving relationship with the God who created you and forgives you of your sins. In that case, you can never have a genuine loving relationship with anyone else. You will continually find fault and blame in others. You will judge them according to who you are rather than who God says they are.

The second commitment is to WORSHIP – the Lord requires our Worship. We are created to worship Him and genuinely have no one and nothing before Him. John 4:24 says, "God is a spirit: and they that worship Him must worship Him in spirit and truth." We were created for one purpose: to worship the Lord! Only the Lord is worthy to be praised. Nobody can do for us what He can and does. Not because we deserve it, but because of who God is and the sacrifice of His son, Jesus, on the cross.

Worshipping God is the heartfelt, daily act of acknowledging His supreme worth, power, and love through obedience, praise, and a surrendered life, rather than just a formal ritual. It is a holistic lifestyle of devotion, often described as "worth-ship," where one aligns their will with God's and expresses gratitude through actions, service, and adoration.

To truly worship is from the heart, it's an internal posture. It's sincere devotion.

How We Worship God:

- **Through singing and music:** Lifting our voices in praise and adoration through songs.

- **Through prayer and thanksgiving:** Speaking directly to God, offering our gratitude and bringing our requests before Him.

- **Through obedience:** Living in alignment with God's will and His Word.

- **Through service:** Serving others as an expression of our worship to God.

- **Through sacrifice and giving:** Offering tithes, our time, or even fasting as a demonstration of our devotion.

- **Through study and meditation:** Reading and reflecting on Scripture to know God more deeply.

Who do you worship? What or whom have you made your god? How much effort does it take to hold on to it? Does it truly return what you invest in it? What occupies your mind? Where is your constant focus?

(Isaiah 26:3) "Thou will keep him in perfect peace, whose mind is stayed on thee… [God]"

When your mind is fixed on Him, you find peace even when everything seems to fall apart, and joy even when others are overwhelmed with frustration.

King David understood this through his own life experiences. In (Psalm 16:11), he declares:

"Thou will show me the path of life: in thy presence is fullness of joy; at thy right hand are pleasures for forever."

In worship, we encounter the fullness of God's grace and His daily blessings. True worship happens when our minds are fully centered on Him, shutting out the distractions and worries of the world. It is in that stillness that we begin to hear His voice. He gives guidance, direction, and answers. Through worship, we receive peace and joy.

The third commitment is **obedience**, and this is where it becomes challenging. Why? Because we often believe we know what is best, what to do, when to do it, and how to do it. This was one of the hardest lessons to grasp, especially when I thought I was doing everything right according to my own standards.

Like children discovering their independence, we sometimes act as though we don't need guidance. We resist instruction, convinced we can manage on our own. In the same way, we can become spiritually defiant—turning away from God's standards and constantly striving to assert our independence.

1 Samuel 15:22 reminds us of the true importance of obedience:

1 Samuel 15:22 the NLT (New Living Translation) But Samuel replied, "What is more pleasing to the Lord: your burnt offerings and sacrifices or your obedience to his voice? Listen! Obedience is better than sacrifice, and submission is better than offering the fat of rams."

Behold, to obey is better than sacrifice. We have been given free will—the choice to follow or not to follow.

He will not change His Word for our comfort.

Jonah's most significant challenge was obeying what he knew was right. God called him to fulfill a purpose. His disobedience was willful and could hardly be more defiant and direct.

God called him twice (Jonah 3:1-2). Once again, the Lord spoke to Jonah. He said, "Go to Nineveh, that great city, and proclaim the message I have given you to the people." How many times has the Lord told you to "GO," launch into the deep, step out into the unknown, challenge the unfamiliar, not in your direction but the direction set before you? Jonah, like us, went, but not in the direction that would bring him success. Fear and disobedience are relatives; they live in the same house together. The unknown, not having control of the outcome, and fear of our predicted outcome can create chaos.

The pattern I followed was to analyze the situation by justifying my reasoning. If I could not control the outcome, I would become anxious, and my anxiety would take over. Jonah had judged the people of Nineveh; he rationalized his decision, took control of the situation, and did it his way, which was to "run." Are you running? Jonah was warned this wasn't going to be easy. He was told to go to a vast city and tell the people about their evil ways. The Lord knew he couldn't go alone; the calling was too big for Jonah. When God calls us to do something beyond our natural ability, we must trust the Lord and lean on him for guidance. Proverbs 3:5-6 tells us how to handle these situations. The NKJV says: "5) Trust in the Lord with all your heart, And lean not on your own understanding; 6) In all your ways acknowledge Him, And He shall direct your paths." He already knows it's too big. When God calls us to his work, we cannot do it without him; he tells us in (Isaiah 55:8). For my thoughts are not your thoughts, neither are your ways my ways." The Lord had told him beforehand that this would be challenging.

The fourth commitment is GIVING - The return of giving is based on a spiritual principle that says that whatever you give, it will be given back to you. However, you must be a cheerful giver to reap the overwhelming rewards of your giving. What holds us back from fulfilling our full potential is "self-will" rather than God's will.

Believe it or not, it starts with giving, but we must provide for the right reasons. God does not need anything from us. It is his way of testing how much we trust him and what we are willing to give up. God arranges the flow of blessings, whether through a job, a marriage, an inheritance, or whatever it may be. However, he requires that we obey the law of giving (2 Corinthians 9:6-7). Still, I say, He which soweth sparingly shall also reap sparingly, and he which soweth bountifully shall reap also bountifully. God loves a cheerful giver. Giving is a significant principle for receiving what God has. (Psalms 29:11) The Lord will give strength unto his people,

37:4 Delight yourself also in the Lord; and he shall give you the desires of your heart, (Luke 6:38) Give and it shall be given back to you, good measure, pressed together, running over, shall men give into your bosom. Our liberality should be just like that. If you want God's best, you have to give your best. When we don't understand this principle, we **The fifth commitment is FAITH – What does God say about having faith?**

Faith is the foundation of our relationship with God. The Bible defines faith as "confidence in what we hope for and assurance about what we do not see" (Hebrew 11:1 It is not just belief. It is active trust in God's Word over our circumstances.

Without faith, it is impossible to please God. (Hebrews 11:6). Faith is what connects us to Him. It is how we receive His grace, walk in His promises, and fulfill His purpose for our lives. We are saved by grace through faith, not by works, so that no one can boast (Ephesians 2:8-9).

Faith is powerful. Jesus teaches that even faith as small as a mustard seed can move mountains (Matthew 17:20). That means it is not the size of your faith that matters. It is where you place it. When your faith is in God, even a little becomes more than enough.

Faith is not passive. It requires action. The Bible tells us that faith without works is dead (James 2:17). True faith shows up in how we live, how we respond, and how we trust God even when things do not make sense. It is choosing to believe God's truth over what we feel, see, or experience.

Faith also requires patience. God's promises are not always immediate, but they are always sure. We inherit those promises through faith and patience. Abraham is a powerful example. He did not waver in unbelief regarding God's promise but was strengthened in faith, giving glory to God (Romans 4:20).

So how do we build faith?

The Word tells us clearly, "Faith comes by hearing, and hearing by the Word of God" (Romans 10:17). The more we hear, read, and meditate on God's Word, the stronger our faith becomes. Faith grows when we stay connected to Him.

Jesus makes this connection clear in John 15:5. "I am the vine; you are the branches. If you remain in me and I in you, you will bear much fruit; apart from me, you can do nothing." Without Him, we are limited, but with Him, all things are possible.

Faith is also expressed through what we speak. When we believe in our hearts and confess God's promises, we align ourselves with His truth. We begin to walk not by sight, but by faith (2 Corinthians 5:7).

This means we do not rely on circumstances to determine what we believe. The answer is not in the situation. The answer is in God. No matter what it looks like, faith stands firm.

Jesus demonstrated this when He spoke about the fig tree and told His disciples that if they had faith and did not doubt, they could speak to a mountain and it would move (Matthew 21:21). God works through faith, even small faith.

The truth is, we cannot take this journey of purpose without faith. What God has called us to do is beyond our natural ability. It is too great for us to accomplish on our own.

Jesus said in John 14:6, "I am the way, the truth, and the life. No one comes to the Father except through me." Everything begins and ends with Him.

If we are going to walk in purpose, we must trust Him completely. We must stand on what we know, not on what we feel. Faith is believing that what God said is true, even when we cannot see it yet.

When we understand faith, believe it, and walk in it with confidence, we position ourselves for God to move in our lives in ways we never imagined.

JONAH

You might ask what all of that has to do with running from God. Not understanding God's principles will lead you in the wrong direction and cause you to pay a severe price. Let's look at it naturally and let your heart tell you the rest. The Lord requires that we love him above all else; he has shown us what true love is (John 3:16). For God so loved the world that he gave his only begotten son (15:17). For God sent not his son into the world to condemn the world, but that through him the world might be saved. Can you give that kind of unconditional love? Do you believe that scripture? If you are going through something you know you cannot fix, it might be time to ask yourself how authentic that scripture is. There is scripture after scripture that defines love, tells us how to love, tells us the fruit of love, and tells us the rewards of love. Because "love" is that important to our Heavenly Father, then that means that He (God) wants "love" to be that important to us.

If we don't understand GOD's kind of love, God will allow us to go through some things, disappointments, hurts, and failures repeatedly if we desire Him in our lives. (Deut. 6:15) For the Lord thy God is a jealous God..." He will not share your affections; He must come first! That was Jonah's first mistake. He didn't understand that his calling required him to have love in his heart for people he didn't want to love. Jonah was just like you and me; he had spiritual ups and downs. He loved God and wanted God to use him and do what God called him to do, but he wanted it on his terms. He tried to pick the place and the RIGHT people. It's not easy to love unlovable people, people who have hurt us, people who deliberately caused pain in our lives, or people who used us.

We judge who God should save and who should be blessed based on who they are and what they have done. We so easily forget how God, by His grace, saved us from our mess, overlooked our faults, and forgave our sins and shortcomings. People don't forget what you have done or what you used to be, but God forgets them. He tells us in (Isaiah 43:25)" I, even, I am he that blotteth out thy transgressions for mine own sake, and will not remember thy sins." Paul writes in (Romans 3:23) "For all have sinned, and come short of the glory of God..." No one has not sinned; we are born into sin, and it's ONLY the grace of God and His love that continually keeps us from going straight to hell. I'm so glad the God I serve is merciful and gracious, that he loves me more than anyone could love me or that I could love myself.

Aren't you?

We are told (Deuteronomy 6:5), "And thou shalt love the Lord thy God with all thine heart, soul, and all thy might." How can we help someone else if we don't trust God to help us and let him control our thoughts and decisions? We are instructed to (Proverbs 4:23)" keep your heart with all diligence; for out of it are the issues of life."

Jonah had issues that prevented him from doing God's work. He had malice in his heart for the people he was supposed to help. Who do you have malice against? Who are you supposed to help? Who are you supposed to take to church? Who are you supposed to love, despite what they have done to you? Who do you need to forgive for what they have done to you, who hurt you, who disappointed you, who mistreated you? His heart was not right, so he could not help the people of Nineveh.

I don't know about you, but I was just like Jonah. God is still working on me; I'm so glad He is. The Lord had to show me my ways. I was judgmental in simple ways that didn't matter; I justified it by saying it's just the way I am. I thought people who didn't work were lazy; they didn't want to work, and I believed that if you wanted to work, you could find work. I never considered what a person might be going through, that they might have barriers that hinder them. I always worked despite my obstacles and had no understanding or little compassion for anyone who struggled due to a lack of employment. I judged from a narrow perspective. Jonah thought the people he was to help; he believed they wanted to live the life they had, so why should he tell them what God wanted? They were too evil to be supported.

How can you believe or accept God's plan for your life if you have a closed mind? We can never accomplish true success without his (God's) intervention. Remember, in (John 15:5) He tells us, "…for without me you can do nothing."

Let's look at Jonah. Jonah was an accredited prophet and a traveling evangelist from Gathhepher near Nazareth. His name means "Dove." Webster's dictionary defines the word "dove" as a noun for peace or the advocate of peace, a peaceful policy. Isn't that what Jonah was commissioned to accomplish in Nineveh? He was to preach the Word of God to restore order to an idolatrous worship city and wicked people who inflicted extreme cruelty on prisoners of war. This was a city on the east bank of the Tigris River, more than 500 miles from Palestine, and they practiced pure wickedness. Nineveh and its surroundings were evil. They had no regard for God or His commandments.

Jonah knew God's voice and had God's mind, but when he was tested with a challenging situation, he realized he didn't trust God.

He was fearful and afraid because of what he knew about the people. The unknown can be frightening and looks impossible, but we have protection.

In Isaiah 43:1 -20, even though the Israelis were unfaithful, He tells them (43:1), "...Fear not, for I have redeemed you; I have summoned you by name, you are mine. When you pass through the waters, I will be with you, and when you pass through the rivers, they will not sweep over you. When you walk through the fire, you will not be burned; the flames will not set you ablaze. For I am the Lord, your God." Even when we don't deserve it, His love for us never changes. We DO NOT have the power or the strength in ourselves to do what God has called us to do. Even when we think we are strong, we are weak; only with God and through God can we do everything!

Jonah 1:1-2 begins with "The word of the Lord came to Jonah's son Amittai; Go to the great city of Nineveh and preach against it because its wickedness has come up before me." Isn't that Jonah's purpose? Jonah's success was guaranteed; his one weapon was God's Word. But Jonah ran. He got in a boat headed to the South of Spain, Tarshish, which was 2000 miles away. You can't run from God; He is everywhere you go. The message was strong, but the city needed to be more significant. Jonah was afraid of what God told him to say. God keeps us and brings us through impossible situations and circumstances. Yet, when He challenges us to trust Him, we waver in our trust and faith. We run from God.

The city of Nineveh, according to historical and archaeological evidence, indicates that in the eighth century BC, the primary city of Nineveh "was probably no more than a mile across at its widest point."

(Baker et al., Obadiah, Jonah, Micah, Intervarsity)

Since a person might walk twenty miles in one day, and Jonah's journey was three days, it is virtually certain that Jonah's ministry included the suburbs of Nineveh.

The message was of repentance, or Nineveh would be overthrown in forty days. God not only controlled the call but also the message. Galatians 1:11-12) Both times, God told Jonah, "Go to the great city of Nineveh and preach…. God would give him the message. It was God's message, not Jonah's, but he focused on the wrong thing. Running comes from a lack of focus and purpose; when we run from God, we run into trouble because we are out of his perfect will for our lives. We bring hardship and pain into our lives and those we care for.

Jonah did not have the commitments, as discussed earlier, to give him that inner strength he needed, the faith to trust and believe in God. Jonah only saw rich, cruel, heartless people who he thought would have killed him. Why Nineveh, they are evil, and I'm afraid. Jonah judged the people in the city, just like us, and made the biggest mistake of his life. Jonah ran out of the city and onto a boat onto the ocean. God knew what Jonah was up against and how people in the city would react, BUT GOD made way for Jonah to do what he asked of him. If Jonah had trusted in the God he served, the One who called him, loved God's people, regardless of what he knew about them, had spent time in Worship, had been willing, given of himself, and had the faith to believe his life would have been different sooner than later. Jonah spent three days in a big fish's belly; can you imagine? The stink, the disgust, the reality was to let Jonah know there is only one way out of your mess, and it's God's way. Have you ever felt like there was no way out of what you're going through?

WHEN WE RUN FROM GOD

Jonah ran from God and himself. He ran out of fear and uncertainty about the situation. He judged the circumstances and judged the people; they were not worthy of being saved; they were, in his eyes, too wicked. He allowed fear and anxiety to rule him and rob him of his peace. Jonah was to have peace in his purpose, which was evident because of what his name represents. The Word tells us to be anxious for nothing, but we are to have peace in all things. Peace comes from faith and trust in God. Jonah's faith was shaken; he wavered in his faith, and he began to disbelieve in God and depended on his thinking.

Jonah was in the right place at the right time, but because he prejudged the situation's outcome, he ran in the wrong direction, like many of us. So often, we run from the very thing that will bring us peace and success.

Jonah had determined that the people were beyond help and too evil to listen to anything good. It seemed impossible because of his thinking and his way of doing things. Whenever we believe something is impossible, it brings a certain level of insecurity and fear. Fear will always cause wrong decisions; it creates a lack of control and soundness of the mind. Whenever fear sets in, the first reaction is to escape the situation, wanting to get out. (Proverbs 29:25) "Fear of man will prove to be a snare, but whoever trusts in the Lord is kept safe." Trusting in God will bring success. 2 Timothy 1:7 says, "God did not give us a spirit of fear but of power, love, and a sound mind." When Jesus told Peter to get out of the boat and come to Him, as long as Peter kept his eyes on Jesus, he didn't remember the impossible. The second he thought about his surroundings, he began to sink. Jonah took his mind off God; he did not trust in Him and ran into a disastrous situation that he could not control, which almost cost him his life. We read that and think, but he made it. Yes, he did, but look at what he went through – three days and the fish's belly, which does not sound like a sunny picnic.

God's timing is perfect, even though it appears that it's the worst possible timing or situation. God allows everything for a reason; He knows what's best for us because He knows more about us than we know about ourselves. God knows the end from the beginning; He knows our weaknesses and strengths before we realize them. I can't tell you how many times I thought God made a mistake; I've felt God couldn't have allowed this situation. He couldn't have wanted me in this mess. There have been so many situations that I ran, thinking this wasn't for me, only to run into worse situations. I didn't allow God's process to take effect. I became discouraged and ready to give up. I have tried myself and become so exhausted that I didn't want to try to work it out and was, at times, almost willing to accept whatever worse fate was going to happen to end the situation.

I lost my peace of mind to such a degree that I thought I was losing my mind. When you run from God, you will run into danger, not necessarily physically, but in all other ways that prevent you from being happy and looking forward to the future without enthusiasm or hope. You will eventually lose all reasoning of a sound mind and focus because there is no direction without Him. We will miss the intended outcome because we can't see it, it doesn't feel right, or it will never end. I have left the situations God directed me to because I felt out of control; I couldn't handle or control them. Jonah couldn't prevent the people in Nineveh, and he wasn't supposed to. He was to do what God told him to do: preach salvation, and God would do the rest.

The answer to "WHEN" with God is when He thinks we are ready. If we know him and trust him, then we know Romans 5:1 -6 tells us, "Therefore, since we have been justified through faith, we have peace with God through our Lord Jesus Christ, through whom we have gained access by faith into this grace in which we now stand. And we rejoice in the hope of the glory of God. Not just in the hope of His glory.

We also rejoice in our suffering because suffering produces perseverance, character, and hope. And hope does not disappoint us because God has poured his love into our hearts by the Holy Spirit he gave us." Why would we run from a victorious process that the Master guarantees? You and I are ready when we have developed God's character, except His love, and trust Him. Trust in God, not because of what we have done or not done, but because God loves us despite ourselves.

Some of the most remarkable men in the bible have run from God; we are not the only ones running. There was a man named Saul, the bible tells us in Acts 8:3: "As for Saul, he made havoc in the church, entering into every house, and having men and women committed to prison. Saul was someone to be feared if you were a Christian, to the point that he went and received permission to persecute Christians. Acts 9:1 "...breathing out threatening and slaughter against the disciples of the Lord, went unto the high priest, and desired of his letter to Damascus to the synagogues, that if he found any on his way, whether they were women or me, he might bring them bound onto Jerusalem". BUT GOD had a plan, plans He had for his life, the same way He has for us. As of Acts 9:3, "Saul was a changed man; he was no longer Saul but became Paul, a mighty man of God." Read the rest of the chapter about how God can change our lives. In an instant, God can make a difference in our lives. Paul was a brilliant scholar and had a position and clout in his mess. God can change anyone!

Jonah was no exception, and neither are we. God can stop us in our tracks whenever He wants to. Although we live in different times, our ways of thinking have not changed. Still, neither has God; Hebrews 13:8, "Jesus Christ the same yesterday and today and forever." He still has the exact requirement; Romans 11:6 tells us that" without FAITH it is impossible to please God," and you can only have faith if you believe He exists. When you think He is what He says He is, then we can endure the trials of life. When we run from God, we are prime candidates to learn about His character and how He loves us and desires us to want Him.

WHY WE RUN FROM GOD

It's straightforward. If we can't see ourselves through God's eyes, we will always believe we are not good enough. We are not the kind of person He wants. We feel we can't be a preacher, teach people about the Word of God, or even have unique gifts to help others. God uses ordinary people; He's not looking for exceptional people because He will make you memorable. All we have to be is willing. He knows exactly what He is doing. He knows who we are, our personality, habits, and ways, good and bad. He also knows how to change and shape us into who He knows we are. We run from God because of our hang-ups, not His. We think because of the things we've done and believe that God wouldn't forgive us, or we're not worthy, in some cases, or not smart enough.

I've heard people say I can't pray like this person or that person; I'm not spiritual enough, and nobody would listen to me. We have many reasons or excuses why we think we can't be soldiers in God's army. I know for a fact that there are people who would listen just to you. People listen to those who can relate to their situations or circumstances and who have been where they are. You may not know how, but He does. He knows who you can help. He already knows how and where He wants to use you.

Some people are lost and lonely that nobody else can reach but you, like you, who have gone through some of the same things you have. He will use our experiences and victories to help others because they are just like us. They look good on the outside, smell good, know how to be perfectly matched from head to toe, and behave like they have it going on with no problems, everything under control, while their life is falling apart. We are not unusual. Since the beginning of time, people have been running from God for the same reasons. They were not feeling good enough or did not want to wait.

Our inadequacy is He's adequacy. Moses is an example of not feeling adequate to serve his purpose. God called Moses three times, and each time, he had an excuse until God finally told Moses that's enough; I know what I'm doing, and you need to stop with the excuses. You have a confidence issue, a self-esteem issue. You think you're not important and what you do for a living is not essential, but who you are and how you make your living is just what the Lord is looking for.

Moses thought he did not speak eloquently enough to talk to people or influence those in high positions. When he was three months old, his mother put him in the river to drift, hoping that someone would find him and take care of him. The Pharaoh, the King of Egypt at that time, gave the order to have every son killed and cast into the river to drown. But God can change the outcome when you aren't aware of what He is doing.

The daughter of the very person who would have taken his life found him and raised him. When Moses was 40, he saw one of his people being beaten, looking around and not seeing anyone. He killed the assailant and hid him. When the situation was discovered, the Pharaoh sought to kill Moses, so he fled. He lived in Midian, an area east of the Gulf of Aqaba or on the Sinai Peninsula, inhabited by nomads.

They took him and Reuel, also known as Jethro, the leader, gave Moses his daughter as his wife. Moses was a plain, simple man. Exodus 3:1 tells us that …" Moses kept the flock of Jethro, his father-in-law..." Moses was a herdsman; he took care of animals. You don't have prestige or an essential position in life for God to use you. While Moses was tending to his herd, the Lord sent an angel to Moses; that's how important Moses was to the Lord. 3:2 ... "And the angel of the Lord appeared unto him in a flame of fire out of the midst of a bush..." God called Moses by name. God knows who you are; you can't hide or run from God. When God told Moses who He was, Moses hid his face; he was afraid to look at God. The Lord told Moses He saw how the people were being mistreated; He heard their cries and felt their sorrows.

He [the Lord] came down to deliver them out of the hands of the Egyptians and bring them into a good land. The Lord told Moses ....3:10, "So now, go. I am sending you to Pharaoh to bring my people, the Israelites, out of Egypt." 1st refusal to accept that he was good enough, Moses answered and said... 3:11

Who am I, that I should go to Pharaoh and bring the Israelites out of Egypt? And God said I will be with you. 2nd objection from Moses, Moses goes on to say in 4:10, "O my Lord, I have never been eloquent, neither in the past nor since you have spoken to your servant, I am slow of speech and tongue." In other words, he felt the Pharaoh could out-think him and out-talk him. Moses finally becomes so anxious that he pleads in 4:13, "Lord, please send someone else."

Another reason people run from God is that He does not come or do it when they think He should. Society is goal-driven by time frames. People limit themselves because of time. We set short-term goals and long-term goals. If the goals are reached, especially if years have passed and we have yet to reach our goals, we don't believe we can achieve them, and we give up and settle for less. The test is to believe even if it seems like nothing is happening. Anything worth having should be worth waiting for. Patience, focus, and endurance will bring results.

I don't know if there is a straight path to success, but I have learned God knows the right path. He will allow us to go down the path more than once to prepare us for what He has for us. Patience is the most difficult trait to acquire. Most people stop trusting in God because they don't want to wait on God's timing. God has the season when things should happen, and He has the exact time within that season. We will remain in the season, but mess up waiting for the right time.

There is complete truth that timing is EVERYTHING. Ecclesiastes 3:1-8 tells us about God's timing. The first verse says

"To everything, there is a season and a time to every purpose under the heaven…it describes in 3:2 – 3:8 all the things to expect in His timing. Whatever God promised you, whatever He put in your heart, He will make it happen if you WAIT on HIM, if you have faith to believe.

An example of not waiting, believing by faith, but not wanting to stay is Abraham, the Bible's Father of Faith, the most remarkable man of faith. God told Abraham he was the Father of many nations, meaning he would be the beginning of a people that would come behind him, who are connected to the promises of GOD.

Abraham lived in Ur of Chaldes, a wealthy, crowded, sophisticated pagan center 220 miles southeast of Baghdad. Abram and his wife Sarai (God later changed their names to Abraham and Sarah to reflect their purpose) left the comfort of their home and friends and followed after the Lord's leading. Sarah was not only Abraham's wife but also his half-sister. Again, God uses everyday people and situations. If you don't remember anything else in this book, I pray you always remember that God doesn't think the way we do. He is God; He can do anything He wants to do.

God tells Abraham about his future in the second verse of the twelfth chapter. Genesis 12:3 says, "I (God) will make you into a great nation, and I will bless you; I will make your name great, and you will be a blessing. 12:3 I will bless those who bless you, and I will curse those who curse you, and all people on earth will be blessed through you." God told this to Abraham when he was seventy-five years old. Can you imagine someone telling you at seventy-five that you're going to be a father, your wife has never conceived a child, AND she is almost as old as you are?

Abraham was just like you and me; he had fears and doubts while having faith. On his journey to greatness, he made some big mistakes. He forgot to trust in God and started trusting in himself and his wife. While on this journey, he went to Egypt, where he lied about his wife to the Pharaoh. He told him she was his sister because he was afraid of being killed. But because God orchestrated this time in his life, He worked it out. The Lord inflicted serious diseases on the Pharaoh and his household because of Abraham's wife, Sarah.

How many times has God spoken to you about your purpose, and you went in the opposite direction and faced all of the consequences, but in the end, God still worked it out for you? You know it was God because it should have ended differently, not to your advantage.

Years later, Abraham still didn't have the child God promised him, so he and his wife thought they would take matters into their own hands, like us. You know how it is when God doesn't come when we think He should; Sarah in 16:1 says, "The Lord has kept me from having children. Go, sleep with my maidservant; perhaps I can build a family through her." Abraham, being the loyal husband,

and in those days, it was acceptable to have relations with servants, had an affair with Hagar. She conceived Ishmael.

I don't know about you, but I have had more Ishmael in my life than I care to remember. In my first marriage, I was 21 and thought I knew what was best for me despite my parents' objections. Although my ex-husband and I are friends today, we had a turbulent marriage. He had just returned from Vietnam. He was adjusting to being back in the United States, struggling to adapt, and started drinking.

I was young, having the time of my life, spoiled, immature, and didn't know how to handle any real difficulties. After two years, we separated and divorced. Although we had some good times, my son is my blessing from the marriage. I knew I should have waited to get married, but like most young women, I thought love was enough to keep us together. I don't know what love was, not the kind of love that makes a marriage stay together. I had parents who would always let me come home, so there were no real consequences to my marriage ending.

I had learned a little from that situation. I met my second husband, a charmer who didn't know how to be in a monogamous relationship, but I thought I could fix that, too. We separated for several years and divorced. After several years of disrespect, that marriage also ended. I didn't know it, but GOD was still with me, and he blessed me again with my daughter. Being hardheaded and defiant, I met my third husband. Although he was a good husband, we didn't have a solid foundation to hold us together so that other people couldn't influence our marriage, and we separated and divorced with no children together.

Everybody runs from God in their own way. I've talked to many people who are uncomfortable going to church because of things in their past. I've spoken to men who used to sell drugs and want to change their lives, but, because of their past, are uncomfortable just going to church. I've talked with women who have had bad relationships and are too embarrassed to come to church. I've spoken with people who have had things happen to them, who still blame themselves and are too ashamed to go to church.

We have all fallen short in one way or another; there is no exception. Anyone who believes they have not sinned is deceiving them self. Everybody has a past or something they would rather forget and not have known. Good news: God knew that and promised never to leave or forsake us. He promises to be our helper and our comforter in times of trouble.

We will be sinners until we leave this earth. I encourage anybody reading this book to know that the past, habits, and shortcomings are not too big or too great for God. He loves us despite ourselves and continues giving us more than one chance to come to Him just AS WE ARE.

He can change everything for good! We can, for a while, but He can change you, me, any circumstance, and any situation so that it becomes a thing of the past. He changes our lives with so much love that we don't have to feel ashamed, sad, or burdened by our mistakes. He (The Lord) doesn't hold our mistakes against us; He is a FORGIVING God. If we could remember that, we would stop beating ourselves up when we mess up.

You might say I haven't done anything bad or wrong, but we need to ask the Lord to forgive us and ourselves for anything that is not good. Here are just a few things that do not please the Lord that we may consider not to be so bad - evil thoughts about another person, envy or jealousy; gossip with your neighbors, not returning the extra change to the cashier, deliberately cutting someone off for a parking space, accepting a job that lacks integrity, lack of discipline in spending, lack of patience, low tolerance, not spending time with family, lousy temper - food for thought!

We can sit in the church every Sunday and still not have time for God or to do what God wants us to do. We all have something that God wants to change in us, big or small; it's all the same to Him. Whatever doesn't make us feel good can keep us from coming to Christ. We must look at ourselves before we look at someone else's faults. Our ways save us from seeking His purpose and plan for our lives. He has a PERFECT plan for you.

THE PAIN OF RUNNING FROM GOD (CONSEQUENCES)

I have learned the price is too high to do it my way since there are unnecessary pains and lifelong consequences. I use the words "pain" and "consequences" because these words describe why life lacks quality and fulfillment according to God's Word.

The Merriam-Webster Dictionary defines them as follows: pain 1. punishment, penalty, 2. suffering or distress of body or mind; consequences 1. result, 2. importance; effect, outcome, significance.

Pain and struggles are not necessarily a sign that we are running from God. Many times, they are allowed by Him for a greater purpose. God uses hardship to refine our faith, build our strength, and draw us into deeper dependence on Him.

Instead of running from pain, we are called to run to God. It is in those difficult moments that we learn to seek Him more, trust Him more, and find comfort in His presence. What feels like pressure is often God shaping us for what lies ahead.

Hardship is part of the refining process. Just as gold is refined by fire, our faith is strengthened through trials. These moments develop perseverance, build character, and produce hope within us. What we go through is not wasted. God uses it to prepare us for His purpose.

Pain also draws us closer to Him. In times of struggle, we are invited to pray, to listen, and to rely on God in ways we often do not when life is easy. He is present in the middle of our suffering, offering peace, strength, and comfort when we need it most.

God also allows suffering because He has given us free will. With the ability to choose comes the possibility of pain, but also the opportunity for real love, growth, and transformation. Even in that, God works all things together for good.

Through suffering, God reveals His power and grace. When we reach the end of our own strength, we begin to depend fully on Him. Our lives then become a testimony to others. People are drawn to God when they see faith that stands strong in the middle of hardship.

There are many reasons God allows suffering in our lives. It shapes us to become more like Christ (Romans 8:17). It teaches us to depend on Him (2 Corinthians 1:9). It helps remove the things in our lives that take His place (1 John 5:21). It equips us to comfort others who are hurting (2 Corinthians 1:4). It reminds us that this world is not our final home (John 15:19). It humbles us and keeps us grounded (2 Corinthians 12:7). It strengthens our faith and endurance (James 1:2-4).

The truth is, we may not always understand why we go through certain things. But we can trust that God does. What we experience now cannot compare to what He has prepared for us.

Pain is temporary, but God's purpose is eternal.

Ultimately, you and I won't know the full reason for our suffering until we get to heaven. At that moment, Jesus will wipe away every tear, and death will be no more. The current suffering that you experience will not be worth comparing to the glory that you'll know in heaven. But, for now, you should expect to suffer. As John Piper once said, "We cannot look at the cross and see Jesus there and think we'll be spared."

There can be personal destruction, a lack of feeling complete, constant fear, self-doubt, and so much more. When we feel insecure about ourselves and our lives, we punish ourselves by denying ourselves happiness and complete fulfillment, and always running, trying to figure it out, always trying something new or different. There needs to be more consistency and stability. There is nothing new under the sun, Ecclesiastes 1:9 tells us, "What has happened before will happen again. What has been done before will be done again. There is nothing new in the world."

Doing the same thing the same way brings the same results. When we have no peace and are in constant distress, there is no stability in our thinking. It's impossible. The mind starts to wander, and thoughts to our disadvantage begin to creep into the mind. If we want peace to know what is good for us, we must do it the Apostle Paul's way, he tells us. Philippians 4:8: "Finally, my brethren, whatsoever things are true, whatsoever things are honest, whatsoever things are just, whatsoever things are pure, whatsoever things are lovely, whatsoever things are of good report, if there be any virtue, and if there be any praise, think on these things…4:9…and the God of peace shall be with you".

Has your lack of peace and confusion caused you to lose some things? What have you lost? Have you lost your joy and happiness? Are you sad and depressed? Are you always tired? What is on your mind? What are you thinking about? Are you pushing people away? Are friends and family avoiding you?

I say "the pain of running from God" because there is order to everything in life, big or small. In our day- to-day lives, we don't think about it until we suffer the consequences. From the time we come into this world, the order is set. Our parents must care for us until we feed ourselves, walk, think for ourselves, etc. If parents don't do their job, babies grow up to be adults who don't know how to love and take proper care of themselves in all the ways we see in our world today. They look for answers in all the wrong places and try to find themselves by getting involved in situations with life-long consequences.

In school, we only get to another grade by obeying the rules. The rules include getting along with classmates, studying, doing homework, and passing tests to move to the next grade - we fail. The proof is the drop-out rate, the high rate of illiteracy in this country, those who can't go beyond minimum wages, poverty, etc.

The pain of running from God holds the same consequences. We never reach our potential, and we miss His blessings for us, not because God doesn't want to give them to us, but because we are not in the place to receive them. Our hearts are not right. We are thinking about all of the wrong things.

We don't have to suffer our shortcomings since God will bring us through and give us the life we desire when we trust Him again.

PEACE IN GOD/SIMPLE ANSWER

Romans 10:1-13 in the New Living Translation Bible tells us: 1) Dear brothers and sisters,[a] the longing of my heart and my prayer to God is for the people of Israel to be saved. 2) I know what enthusiasm they have for God, but it is misdirected zeal. 3) For they don't understand God's way of making people right with Himself. Refusing to accept God's way, they cling to their own way of getting right with God by trying to keep the law. 4) For Christ has already accomplished the purpose for which the law was given.[b] As a result, all who believe in him are made right with God.

Salvation Is for Everyone

5) Moses writes that the law's way of making a person right with God requires obedience to all of its commands.[c] 6) But faith's way of getting right with God says, "Don't say in your heart, 'Who will go up to heaven?' (to bring Christ down to earth). 7) And don't say, 'Who will go down to the place of the dead?' (to bring Christ back to life again)." 8) In fact, it says, "The message is very close at hand; it is on your lips and in your heart."[d]

And that message is the very message about faith that we preach: 9) If you openly declare that Jesus is Lord and believe in your heart that God raised him from the dead, you will be saved. 10) For it is by believing in your heart that you are made right with God, and it is by openly declaring your faith that you are saved. 11 As the Scriptures tell us, "Anyone who trusts in him will never be disgraced."[e] 12) Jew and Gentile[f] are the same in this respect. They have the same Lord, who gives generously to all who call on him. 13) For "Everyone who calls on the name of the Lord will be saved."[g]Establish a personal relationship with Jesus, the best thing you could ever do! Tell Him your problems, hurts, disappointments, desires, wants, and needs, then trust Him to see you through. He may not fix every obstacle, situation, circumstance, hurdle, and stumbling block the way you want it fixed, but He WILL see you through it. He will give you peace beyond understanding. The Bible says this: (Philippians 4:6-7) "Do not be anxious about anything, but in everything by prayer and supplication with thanksgiving let your requests be made known to God. And the peace of God, which surpasses all understanding, will guard your hearts and minds in Christ Jesus."

After you've tried everything else, the best thing you can do when you are filled with anxiety and worry is to find a quiet place to pray, find scriptures of peace, and listen to encouraging worship music. God wants you to live a life to the fullest, including having peace and being at peace!

You can have joy when there is no reason; God is building you up, testing your faith; do you trust Him? (James 1:2-4) "2) Count it all joy, my brothers,[b] when you meet trials of various kinds, 3) for you know that the testing of your faith produces steadfastness. 4) And let steadfastness have its full effect, that you may be perfect and complete, lacking in nothing."

When you feel your strength is gone, you can't find strength or joy: you can't do it, but God can," He gives strength to the weary and increases the power of the weak" (Isaiah 40:29).

Nehemiah tells us to enjoy yourself even when it's hard, and you feel too weak to try: "Go and enjoy choice food and sweet drinks (juice), and send some to those who have nothing prepared. This day is holy to our Lord. Do not grieve, for the joy of the Lord is your strength." (Nehemiah 8:10)

It doesn't matter where you are. Paul, the Apostle, had an experience that could have made him feel superior and overbearing, but God, all-knowing and wise, knew how to ensure Paul relied on God's strength and not his own. Corinthians 12:7-10 "7) Now to each one the manifestation of the Spirit is given for the common good. 8) To one there is given through the Spirit a message of wisdom, to another a message of knowledge by means of the same Spirit, 9) to another faith by the same Spirit, to another gifts of healing by that one Spirit, 10) to another miraculous powers, to another prophecy, to another distinguishing between spirits, to another speaking in different kinds of tongues,[a] and to still another the interpretation of tongues.[b] If you want a life of confidence whereby you know beyond a shadow of a doubt you will make it, there will be struggles, but with God's peace in the middle of every storm and just life, consider John 10:10 "The thief (Devil) comes only to steal and kill and destroy; I (Jesus) came that they may have life, and have it abundantly" (John 10:10).

Romans 10:1-13 in the New American Standard Bible describes salvation like this: The Word of Faith Brings Salvation

1. Brothers and sisters, my heart's desire and my prayer to God for them is for their salvation.

2. For I testify about them that they have a zeal for God, but not in accordance with knowledge.

3. For not knowing about God's righteousness and seeking to establish their own, they did not subject themselves to the righteousness of God.

4. For Christ is the [a]end of the Law for righteousness to everyone who believes.

5. For Moses writes of the righteousness that is [b]based on the Law, that the person who performs [c]them will live by [d]them.

6. But the righteousness [e]based on faith speaks as follows: "Do not say in your heart, 'Who will go up into heaven?' (that is, to bring Christ down),

7. or 'Who will descend into the abyss?' (that is, to bring Christ up from the dead)."

8. But what does it say? "The word is near you, in your mouth and in your heart"—that is, the word of faith which we are preaching,

9. [f]that if you confess with your mouth Jesus as Lord, and believe in your heart that God raised Him from the dead, you will be saved;

10. for with the heart a person believes, [g]resulting in righteousness, and with the mouth he confesses, [h]resulting in salvation.

11. For the Scripture says, "Whoever believes in Him will not be [i]put to shame."

12. For there is no distinction between Jew and Greek; for the same Lord is Lord of all, abounding in riches for all who call on Him;

13. for "Everyone who calls on the name of the Lord will be saved."

THAT IF YOU CONFESS WITH YOUR MOUTH, "JESUS IS LORD," AND BELIEVE IN YOUR HEART THAT GOD RAISED HIM FROM THE DEAD, YOU WILL BE SAVED.

- ROMANS 10:9